John Whale

# *Waterloo Teeth*

T0168189

*Northern House*

CARCANET

First published in Great Britain in 2010 by
Northern House
In association with Carcanet Press Limited
Alliance House
Cross Street
Manchester M2 7 AQ

A CIP record for this book is available from the British Library
ISBN 978 1 84777 111 7

The publisher acknowledges financial assistance from Arts Council England

Typeset by XL Publishing Services, Tiverton
Printed and bound in England by SRP Ltd, Exeter

# Contents

# Acknowledgements

I am grateful to the editors of the following magazines and anthologies in which some of these poems – or versions of them – have appeared: *Anvil New Poets 2, Black Box Manifold, British Journal of Eighteenth-century Studies, The Independent, Interchange, Kunapipi, Ninth Wave, The North, Poetry and Audience, Stand, The Tempest,* and *Versus.* 'Salt Fish Stories' was a prize-winner in the Yorkshire Poetry Competition. 'The Nondescript' appeared in the *National Poetry Competition Prizewinners' Anthology.* 'Kynance Cove Again' was broadcast on BBC Radio Leeds as part of National Poetry Day in 1996.

# The Invertebrate Zenith

*O for a life of sensations ...*

In the soft name of science
this is the place for poetry.
At the invertebrate zenith
shaming the arid cameleon
with the most unpoetical
of all God's creatures,
this one fine specimen of
the *octopus dofleini*.

It has no rigid form, no
back-boned articulation –
just three pumping hearts
and the most talented epidermis
known to man, and a second
'touch memory' which isn't.
Fantastic elastic cephalopod
you can crawl, walk or swim,
and your chromatophores command
immediate volcanic change.
Your lost limbs return like phantoms
and like phantoms change their form
to suit the various functions
of the three short years to
all-out molluscan surge.

You are not part of this screening
and we have no anaesthetic.
You convulse with scarlet pain
at the touch of this philosophy.
Your bubbling tears dissolve
under the poet's ruthless lens.
My bleached linen cuffs
are like blotting paper.
Piss your unprintable ink.

# Token

Look down upon this little child.
Suffer it to come before you.
See it clutch a sailor's button,
or a thimble scratched with kisses.
A necklace of blood-red coral.
A hazelnut notched with a knife.
Take away all these tell-tale signs,
all the stones which lead back home.

We carried it along our veins.
From the frets, cold sweats and fevers
(those things that they'd come through)
the immunity of our lost parents.
But in our words and in our manners,
in our dress and in our prayers,
we were someone else's children.
It was the things not there and bare
which marked us out as foundling.

I have no one thing from her hand:
no sign of her finger's end or nerve,
the unmistakable print of her
as the blunted nib of her pen
in her hand (or someone else's)
forms all these characters together:
*You have my heart tho' we must part.*
I squeeze my imaginary flake
of mother-of-pearl. Hold it up.
See how her face blends with mine.

# Mary Toft

My child pulled itself away from me
in the dark fold of my bruised womb.
I could not see him in my rush of blood,
the confusion of my flesh and bone.

In the first green months of my term
I craved the milky meat of a rabbit
its silky pinkness bruised with blue,
the sharp white fracture of a bone

as small as any rodent might produce.
And then I decided to seek him out,
racing each one, this way and that,
my chest scorched on the far pasture.

And I never came close enough to stroke
or catch a glimpse of his unformed face.
That night I dreamed of a rabbit in my lap,
its legs kicking hard against my thighs.

In deep December I sent for Howard
who delivered me safely of a limp buck.
And I had him back day after painful day
until a pile of eight (all dead) lay

stacked upon the linen bedding.
When the others came to watch:
famed Manningham and St Andre,
I managed nearly seventeen in all,

but most of these were incomplete,
some lacked fur and some the bone,
some were laces of silver sinew,
some mere tags to load a barley stew.

They removed from one a tiny lung
which looked like a fairy-sponge
I'd once seen beached in stormy Kent,
and sliced it lengthwise, wafer-thin.

And the upshot of all their musings
was my boy had once sucked vital air –
that gas with neither taste nor smell
he could not breathe inside my womb.

After all my stale confinements,
I think of him now alive on the down
where the wild thyme scents the turf
in a fold of the winterbourne coomb.

# Whistlejacket

I will lay to in my most rational method.
At eight and a half I could dissect a dog
and anatomize a pregnant hare.
I did it in the din of my father's shambles,
in the thick stench of his curing yards.
I cherished each dead mare I drained.
I sent hot tallow along the exact course
of all her pink and purple vessels
as if it were the milk of human kindness.
And as she floated from the roof-beam's teagle
I heard her hoof-tips tick the flagged floor.
There was no time to be lost. I undressed
the membranes of her peritoneum and pleura
and relieved her of all her baggy guts and lungs.
I worked in the coldest months with vinegar
and scribbled down notes at every stage.
I have drawn the demon's claws on a filly's back.
I have exposed the human form divine
with that of the tiger and the common fowl.
Now I've removed all trace of boots, bridle
and the pride of the Rockingham Whigs.
At last, I've boiled it down to this:
taut tawny grace on an earthy ground,
pure horse in all its own space.


## II


To know the horse I work back to bone.
I will remove the well-groomed mane,
the plaited tail and the ribbon'd fringe.
The velvet flesh of the lower head
sticks tight as any lady's glove.
The skin falls off without demur
this beast so fabulously blue and pink,
its inner coils rippling in the tide,
its lungs like South Sea sponges,

its wasted teeth of revealed coral.
When whalers stand aboard their carcasses
and slice through flesh to fresh baleen
they work their way back down the bone
so that they can distil it all to ambergris:
to light a city's lamps and studios.
And I will assemble the polished bones,
start out now from scratch to find
the invisible genius of the horse.

# Fresh Hands

When he appeared before anatomists
he insisted on full formal dress,
and when he touched their Scottish beef
he made sure he used fresh hands.
Burke the butcher, Hare the thief.
The former came past grief to the slab
As did all the ripe and dripping oddities
diverted from the fishwives of the Forth.
Burke's own convulsive ventricles collapsed
with those of smiling sharks, bonitos
and kindly, bottle-nosed dolphins.
Intent on the precise arrangements
of teeth, Knox revised the name
of the lazy-eyed Koala Bear
to the less cuddly Wombat of Flinders.
He performed a similar service for
the sad dugong, the sliced manatee,
and the soo-soo of the milky Ganges.
Dead-shot Knox straddled his Arab mare
as only a man can who's written
a paper on the nostrils of a horse,
as one who can pronounce with certainty
that the hillock of the African termite
is more remarkable than the Pyramids.
Desperate to preserve the races of Man,
Knox the scrubbed Englishman went off
to meet the South African carnivora
refusing to concede that the laughing hyena
is a profoundly social animal,
an oversight which one-eyed Knox –
whose perfect eye was perfection itself –
can be forgiven when compared with
the ease with which he assumed
the call-girls and the desperate beggars
of Edinburgh fell without a struggle
into the fresh hands of Burke and Hare.

# Brioche

*Qu'ils mangent de la brioche.*
(Attributed to Marie-Antoinette.)

She lay beneath the stomach of the king.
A slight rustle inside her. Then nothing.
He charged through his beloved Fontainebleau,
a trail of broken bracken in his wake.

She turned herself over and tried hard to sleep,
to dream of an island crowned with poplars
and breakfast surrounded by ribboned cows,
the deep orange yolks of her darling hens.

She flexed her tense feet down in the sheets
and her toe-nails seemed strangely sharp,
her downy shins felt scaly and rough.
Her shoulders sprouted little leathery wings,

a barb and tail curled out from her behind
and her claws walked off to play with the dauphin.
She felt the stones in her necklace tighten
as they promised to fricassee her liver.

When she struggled hard to say nothing
they forced the common little word brioche
out of her harpy mouth and showered the crowds
with the crumbs of the blood they wanted.

# 1790s Diary

At 2 oclock this Afternoon I buried Poor Lydia Betts.
I did not know she was ill, until she was Dead.
Snip, Fly and Spring cornered and Killed a fine Hare
out on the far Pasture. She tasted well!
By the Papers a very great Rebellion in France.
Veal Collops, Calfs Fry and a boiled Bullock's Heart.

So bitter cold! I had my worn Bay-Mare,
old Peggy, shot before I came downstairs.
I had her Skinned as I intend to have her tanned.
It was an Act of Charity to do as I have done.
A Juicy Tench, Pigeon Pye and a Hashed Calfs Head.

Young Fly ran off with Betty Cary's Mutton
undressed, and eat it all up. A Great Commotion.
I had the Hound hanged this Evening.
The News is the King and Queen of France
carried back to Paris, and on Lloyd's Paper.
Veal rosted, Stewed Eels, two Fellfares and a Blackbird.

My Eye healed. Thank God! I did it by the Tail
of my black Tom Cat. Dreadful times ahead.
The cruel Blood-Thirsty French have killed their King.
God save the Queen, 2 children and their Aunt.
Piggs Face, Green Goose and Giblet Soup.

## A moi, ma chère amie

### I

He sits in his shoe-shaped bath,
relieving midsummer madness
in his psoriacal skin
as it erupts across the *maquis*
of his scrubbed chest.
His tired right arm flops over
the side of the tide-marked tub
and his nib grazes the porphyry.
I see a version of himself
floating above his furred stomach,
his flesh luminous and painfully pink,
as a sworled drop of black ink
smokes itself away into the flesh-warmed water.
He regards his famous ermine scarf
gripping the top of the chair opposite.
I know how he glories in rudeness,
but he's arranged himself quite properly
for my visit – *that striking girl from Caen.*
The green ribbons on my sporty black hat
flutter in the draught as the word *amie*
gives way to a jet of arterial blood
and a cry to burst all the bubbles.
Down on the boulevard
revolutionary lovers
sip at their flesh-flecked *limonades.*

### II

On the midsummer air my soul
soars free of its inflamed skin
like an airship over the body politic.
I am the sacred heart of Marat
shed for you and for everyone else
to nourish the great wheatfields of France.

Down in *l'Église de Cordeliers* the ballast
of my rotting corpse slews in a bath
four women stagger to keep aloft
in a shower of vinegar and strong perfume.
My wound, like an extra mouth,
gapes just wide enough to shock.
My tongue wobbles, but can no longer loll.
The anonymous arm which dropped to the floor
gripping the pen, rights itself in time,
and the choirboys' mouths are full of Gluck
as my actual heart slips like soap
inside an agate urn which swings
high above the swooning crowd.

## Lines on the Death of Mary Wollstonecraft

It is twenty minutes before eight.
Downstairs, they lower their voices
and use two hands to open doors.
A plate chinks in the parlour.
A broom is sweeping the yard.
Fires flare silently into life
and the very air is muffled
with a clear understanding.
Objects in the grey room take on
the familiar shape of objects.
Outside, the cabs and carriages
on their way through the dust
rattle the cobbles with a sound
which is neither midsummer
nor the dead of winter.
In the room below, light
breaks like a stick of chalk
on a table set for two.

Room after room, door after door,
I search the house through
and come up with nothing.
Nothing touched it seems by her
as she went reeling through life.
And it took so many days to die.
I take her brave book of letters
which suits this frozen north
that grips the edges of my mind.
Her spirit melts happiness
to nothing less than true content.
Through my gloom of innumerable pines
a waterfall jumps the darkness
and its voice suddenly aches,
aches with a weight of water
flowing under Putney Bridge.
I imagine her ghostly skirt
billowing in the cold Norwegian sea.

But she is striking out for life
alone on the wide ocean.
Before her floats a veil or gauze,
a cold transparent envelope
of water thickened into life
and marked for life with rings
like bloodstains in the snow.
It trails purple ribbons.
As my tears salt the sparkling waves
I begin to see through her bright I
as it meets the cold light of day.
Somewhere in the near distance,
a new-born baby starts to cry.
It is twenty minutes before eight.

# The Queen of France

When each new tide brought only bladder-wrack
and brown rubber fronds of deep-sea kelp
into the haven of his native bay,
he kept his lonely watch upon the strand.
Days when a thousand eyes danced on the water,
when the sea lay like glass under heaven,
and the spotless gannet closed white wings
and dropped like a blade through the film.
Days when the swell lashed the local slips
and buried Slea Head in ancient darkness,
when the dancing petrel braved the storm
through troughs of night-time breakers,
and the huddled auks kept guard upon the cliffs.
He kept his watch upon the strand.

When he saw her just above the horizon,
his heart beat like a bird caught in his hands.
She glittered like the morning-star
and a stack of Kerry diamonds.
Then was there a path of gold in Dingle Bay.
He heard what he thought could only be rain,
dripping next to his head on the stone pillow,
and in the roar of waves below he made out
the sound of confused peewits flapping
in the darkness, and the sad-eyed seal
screaming for the life of her departed pups.
The empty house sits snug in Dingle town
as clean and as safe as any palace.
Star-gazy mackerel throng the tormented sea.

# Waterloo Teeth

After Soult and Ney and the Imperial Guard
had gone down among the rotting corn,
we fell upon the rain-soaked bodies of the dead
and ripped lace gorgettes from the dandy officers.
From the rosy cheeks of English plough-boys
we pulled two hundred sets of perfect teeth.

Chalky moonlight kisses the domed pavilion
and turns the Sussex stone to ivory.
Inside, the giddy lovers lose themselves
in chiaroscuro and entangled chinoiserie.
Their tongues explore the sea-horse, walrus
and hippopotamus which grips their foreign teeth.

I conquered all Europe with my attitudes:
Daphne, Miranda, Sibyl, Bacchante.
I sent men's names through the world's loud mouth.
But when I was only poor young Emma Hart,
I took my self to pawn, again and again,
rather than sell my unbroken lines of delicate teeth.

Please don't make your Waterloo eyes at me –
as if there's a world beyond the moon.
All day I dream of Freddy drenched in Flanders.
So when you ask me again how old I am,
I'll purse my lips and make these words your rhyme:
*the same age as my tongue, a little older than my teeth.*

# Internees

They turned in, and in on themselves,
gouging anything that came to hand
in the doldrums of their days.
Lacking whale-tooth, walrus-tusk,
or brilliantly tanned shagreen,
their clean-sucked mutton-bones
became full-blown sloops and
the cathedrals of their native France.

Under their breath they kept Her alive
with baffled shouts of *Vive L'Empéreur!*
as the razor'd bone sliced home
and removed the tiny putty heads
of their compliant aristocrats.

*So much for idle scrimshaw work,*
*scrimshankers, and scurvy sailors.*
He refused such mannikins.
Instead of going miniature
he turned into himself
all the enemy could throw at him:
the insipid *potage de jour*,
the mutton joints complete with bone,
live rats, dogs, and cats,
as he swallowed hard in honour
of Napoleon, his fabled words of Empire,
the Army, and the marching stomach.

# Tom Paine's Bones

*the times that try men's souls*


On a close September night at New Rochelle
Peter Porcupine nuzzles the moist earth.
His spade scrapes grit, sucks at clay, humus,
the tamped remains of Thomas Paine, deist.

The absurdity of legislating beyond the grave
and for it. Cobbett lands at Liverpool
deep in trouble with his bag of bones:
a skeleton to set the kingdom alight.

But with the roast beef of England
hacked down by yeomen at Peterloo
the moment is lost when the scattered bones
could sing and blossom into Liberty tree.

The *droits de l'homme* and the rites of death
chanced in the feverish Luxembourg
when the chalked door opened out not in
and the destroying angel passed him by.

*Man has no property in man,* he wrote,
but his jawbone rattled in a nursery.
Other parts were written off as non-assets
or safely dumped into the Mersey ooze.

Dirty little atheist, shuddered Roosevelt.
Reagan forgets, checks, and has old Tom Paine
born again on auto-cue: *We have it in our power,*
he smiles, *to remake the world anew.*

## The Goree

When the Goree went up in 1802
the rum-soaked flakes sent cattle
reeling through the floodlit crops.
You could see angels flaming in the sky
all the way to Warrington.


*Over the many-languaged*
*town of Liverpool,*
*all heaven was ablaze.*


You'd have to go a long way south
through blistering siroccos
and choking sahel dust
to find a night as close as this.
It must be more than cotton.


It must be more than cotton.

# Sugar

The crisp edge of the white cube
gave way slowly against his palate
and the sweet melt spilling over
teeth on either side of his tongue
like a coolness or spreading heat
(it was always impossible to tell)
suddenly didn't happen at all.
There was instead a thickness,
a gelatinous resistance pulling
the tip of his tongue towards it,
and where the sweetness should be,
not exactly a bitterness as such,
not like the yellow staining glob
of serum which made him salivate
and wince in the crowded clinic
way back in sixties Liverpool –
no, there was a thickness in this
which tasted salty first then sweet,
like the cuts he'd licked in boyhood,
from his own elbows and knees,
and now the sugar came home to him
with all the dark taint of molasses,
the smell drifting from Tate & Lyle,
and the remembered difficulty he'd had
understanding their tins of *Golden Syrup* –
the small cloud of flies gathering
over the body of a dead lion
and the wisdom of the quoted words:
OUT OF THE STRONG
CAME FORTH SWEETNESS.
But all he could think of was the juices
draining inside the rotting carcass,
laid out under an African sun,
and that sickly smell carried on the wind
which seemed to him much more than sugar
and, somehow, very close to home.

# The Mole of Edge Hill

*They called him the King or Mole.*
*He paid teams of grateful navvies*
*to work in worthless circles,*
*and he answered the muttered complaints*
*of weary tenants, by exploding*
*up through their kitchen floors.*
*He elevated humble tunnelling*
*to the status of a polite art*
*and himself to the title of Archbishop.*
*The eleven-year-old with a tin trunk of clothes*
*made a mint out of tobacco*
*and a honeycomb of Edge Hill.*
*At his wedding, he chose hunting-pink*
*and left with a loud halloo*
*to ride to his favourite hounds.*


Dad's words made the streets familiar.
Our city had another, phantom life
which lay beneath our feet.
It ran through secret corridors
which squared the deadly Atlantic,
through crowded, land-mined cinemas,
*and way back before the War*
through dripping sandstone tunnels
scooped by men who begged for work.
We skimmed the catalogue of the dead
which ghosted the famous cuttings
and, in our sleep, we were pursued
by the elusive Spring-Heeled Jack,
who ate up the streets of Everton
with his blood-stained A–Z.

## Salt Fish Stories

### I

All Saturday night the salt fish
leaked its brine into the soaking-pan
and the arched fillet gave off
minute flecks of slow-dissolving flesh.
Its bulk rises silently to a phantom life.
By Sunday morning what was once
faceless, straw-coloured stiff
flops in a rich scum on the ring.
Served new-risen with the bacon fat,
buttercup flesh in perfect shields.

### II

Nosing the current off Newfoundland
the large-eyed, whiskery cod-head
fingers the edge of the continental shelf,
its missing flanks sliced, dried and casked.

### III

Trace the black lines down
through the geometric 'sixties
zig-zag on the formica table-top
to cross-overs, collisions and
the darker triangular dead-ends,
the trails of muddled heroes
caught in a strange breakfast
of war and comics, and comic homely war,
a warm emulsion of fish
lubricating the harsh tang of salt.

One great athletic uncle who
raced Buffalo Bill on foot and won.
*And him on a horse as well!*
Incapable of following Rorke's Drift
in *The Hotspur's* wordy anniversaries,
*The Hurricane's Gott in Himmel!*
*Banzai! Banzai! Zeros at 12 o'clock!*
the ex-boss with a stomach full of glass,
Szenna's heroic crawl across the icy Baltic
or poor young Hughie lost at Anzio.

The budgie rattles in the Anderson
with grans, aunts, uncles, dogs and cats.
The sheer extravagance of oranges.
A mouth soused in deep Atlantic.

# Mam Cymru

She babbled like a girl
of green fields and greener water
pouring through the swillies
of the Menai Straits, of Will Pen Bont,
and old men whose nods and winks
kept watch over the distant Skerries,
of Gwilym choking in the cruel salt current,
of Britain's longest place-name
stammering to its deathly close
in llantysiliogogogoch.
*Mam. Mam. Speak to me mam,*
*in English like yourself.*
She spoke out of her girlhood
to her three exhausted daughters,
as if they were total strangers,
from the time before the century turned,
and she with it into a woman
barely twelve years old,
of the time before she landed
at the Pier Head with little English
to work in big house service,
and heard through the rare accent
that familiar sound she made herself
on the back of her own soft palate.
*Speak. Speak. gogogoch*

# On Porthmeor Beach

No Atlantic breakers
thump and sizzle
in the eyes and minds
of the three young girls
hunched in the sand
of Porthmeor Beach
who face away from us
all well wrapped up
on a calm, calm day
in Whistler's sketch
where the actual sand
of Porthmeor Beach,
grain by irritating grain,
has found its way into
his sworls of oil
as it did in the cold basin
of our guest-house,
in the hollows of our toes,
and in the sills
of our scrapped cars,
long after it was possible
to recall the voices
on Porthmeor Beach
heard only in the gaps
of the booming surf
and through the flooded lids
of my sun-filled eyes.

# Kynance Cove Again

At Kynance Cove the breakers hit you
slap in the chest, and then again
from sparkling stacks of serpentine.

If you go down to Kynance Cove
time your climb to the cliff's foot.
You really need to watch the tides.

You can come back from Kynance Cove.
There's another way if the tide is in:
past the dead thrift and the dwarf furze.

I'm telling you all this because
I know you've been to Kynance once before,
and you know that it's a sacred place

and because I'm choosing to imagine
that one of these three ravens
croaking and stumbling at the cliff top

reminds me of my paternal grandfather
whose chest gave way in the fifties,
almost two years before I was born.

# Reading Aloud

It's my voice in your room again
sounding the air above your shut eyes
and the regular pauses of your breath.
The words perform their usual ministry,
pulling you out of thought and into sleep
until you're on the edge of the realm of sound,
and bound to wake the second the reading stops;
I'm bound now to go on to the story's end,
to find my way out of the haunted forest
of my childhood: the unspeakable hut
whose own chicken legs speak of butchery,
the domestic prisoners who call on me
with their gift of tongues: the charming cat,
the squealing gate and the lashed birches,
the iron teeth which grate upon themselves
and churn the communion of jam and bread
into a shapeless, bloody mess.
I know I can't get back to my beginning
by picking up each thumbed ball of dough –
just white enough in the light of the moon –
each stone sufficiently smooth for the stars;
and now that we've got beyond the hollow
chock of the log swinging in the forest
which sounds to Gretel's ears like
the familiar axe biting the stump
to suggest that her dad's still here;
now that we've heard the click of heels
across the old woman's icing-sugar floor,
the familiar smell of her large bread oven,

I'm close to the end, helped only by
my friends the speaking birds who grace
each frost-sprinkled tuft of cottage
with their pert, bright-eyed knowledge
(having eaten all the evidence)
of the impossible way back home
across the impassable river,
through fog and this surrounding darkness
to the voice which reads to me
so slowly: *Once upon a time*

# Cwm Idwal

We rise through the clouds
on a path of polished stones
past outcrops of wet-look quartz
which could be traces of snowfall
or the lime of a silent raptor
marking time on the empty scree.
We stop at an old iron gate which
squeals and clamps shut on the cwm.

Drizzle spatters the bleak shingle
and trout flip in the shallow lake.
Across the drab tussocks of sheep's fescue
and the inevitable morainic deposits
you can just make out, at the end of the cwm,
climbers stretched on the Idwal Slabs
and, beneath your feet, butterworts and sundews
slowly digesting the summer's flies.

You can wait over a thousand years
for vegetation to reach a climax
and they are measuring time in the cwm.
We return clockwise to the squealing gate
and are about to go back over the lip
when a red thing no bigger than a bird
explodes down the Nant Ffrancon and is gone.
We are locked into this sudden quiet.

# Portbou

*It is more difficult to honour the memory*
*of the nameless than that of the renowned.*

Where the spine of the Pyrenees
buckles in the cool Mediterranean,
and where the idling rolling stock
of the French and Spanish railways
squeals through chilly labyrinths
across a derelict, unpoliced border,
there's a casual car park on the cliff
near a classically upright cypressus
and a tiled portico to the graveyard.
Here, a girdered orange line of steel
cuts through dust and shattered rock
and takes your eyes to a six-foot frame –
something between a coffin and a door –
and no sooner have you entered than
you're made to stand there like an angel
looking down a flight of shining steps
to a shimmering tablet of cobalt light
which, you find, is the sea, the real sea;
but as you try to make your way
you find your path is blocked by glass
and on this glass is etched a thought
on the nature of history and the nameless
which the man himself had penned.
And the steps you cannot take go down
to a sea which none of us will reach,
though we can watch how first it smashes
then licks up the crashing stars below.

## Star Whispers

Our stones screamed across the lake
and we replayed, again and again,
the man who went out across the ice
in silence: a memory to himself.
It was impossible to imagine
the star whispers of his dying breath.

Our stones whistle across the lake
as if the air held wires.
A hunched grey silhouette
is really a starving kingfisher,
and the friend looming out of the fog
has not crossed my mind for months.

# On a Beach in Co. Kerry

We found it in a dip of the dune,
its head held high, still loaded for flight,
the last threads of flesh glued to its wings,
its bleached lower mandible
snagged in the blue and silver arteries
of the glistening fishing nets.
We felt along the grooved palate,
removing the irritable grains
where once the wriggle of sand-eels
and the beating of minute fins
sent shock-waves through its chalky coverts
and along its sulphur-sprinkled neck.
We emptied the eye-sockets
of sand and shells, and looked through
three small, drilled holes to the chamber
which housed enough brain to plunge
beak down, a hundred feet,
eyes fixed on a spinning shoal,
and time the fold of the ink-dipped wings
to break the surface tension of the ocean,
clean and sure: a beak-loaded brain.

From a stony creek in the next bay,
St Brendan set out for his New World
and we wondered at his coracle,
the lack of charts, and a brain
fit for the purpose.

# Calentures

## I

He was all at sea
when dugongs lolled in a lagoon
of vetch and purple clover.

He was beside himself
when the wind shook the breaking waves
into drops of golden barley.

When dolphins tore through scented beds
of asphodel and camomile
he went completely overboard.

## II

When the first motorway went north
it cut his blessed fields in two
and gave him all the time he needed
to sit and watch his fatt'nin beasts.
He'd go out across his concrete bridge
and leave his waving fields for market.
He went as far as Newark in the east.
He went as far as Derby in the south.
In all his life he never saw the sea.
After the death of mother, father, brothers,
he sat alone in the bare room thinking
of the fire he'd kindle with blank cheques.
And some days after he died all alone
they found the cattle moaning at the moon,
and a stack of chairs reaching to the stars.

# Unknown Regions

*He has a thirst for travelling; perhaps he may turn out a Bruce or a Mungo Park … he said he should prefer not to know the sources of the Nile, and that there should be some unknown regions preserved as hunting-grounds for the poetic imagination.* George Eliot, *Middlemarch*

I

*Source of the Nile*

Irritable curiosity drove him to it.
Across the blinding Nubian desert
he kept his eyes fixed on the stars
and saw a horde of Saharan Visigoths

flying before the first simoon,
met the tribe who fed exclusively on lion
and ate beef sliced from the live flank.
The laird was drugged on Ethiopian bream.

If the third cataract left him speechless,
the Nile's source brought him to his knees.
Jupiter stood above the mountains of Geesh
and the quicksilver rose twenty-two inches.

*But grief rolled upon me like a torrent.*
Attacked by a clear case of the horrors
he made oat-cakes out of wild grasses
and bathed himself in the streams of Clyde.

From the confusion of Abyssinian tongues
and the din of bloody courtly battles
he recalled the princess Ozoro Esther
screaming in the metropolis of Gondar.

In his inaudible dreams the roar of waters
drowned the workmen forging his obelisk,
his name adrift in a sea of hieroglyphs
above the Carron's newest smelting-plant.

## II
### *The Eye of Providence*

Nearly five hundred miles
from the nearest settlement,
robbed, stripped and
surrounded by lions

my eye was irresistibly caught
by the beauty of a small moss,
its delicate conformation
of roots, leaves and capsula.

# Surimono

## I

Old men cough and groan on the sheet of snow
which might have brought them to my door.
This is no night for lovers young or old.
The river taxis have frozen into their moorings
and their flickering lanterns go out one by one.
The geese cut an oblique poem in the heavens
and honk at the pent-up inhabitants of Edo.
A lone palanquin flutters along the embankment
and I see that its two busy, faceless bearers
carry nothing but a cold grey square of sky
which forces itself through my circular window.
On that soft cushion sat my ten years patron.
On those same silks I can feel his softer touch.
I look down on my cats, snug in one another's fur.
My mouth-rinsing bowl sits in the window like a blue heart
and I squeeze the wad of tissues at my right hand.

Still in the window
like the blue heart
of its owner,
as crisply drawn
as her folded kimono
or the calligraphic
skeins of geese
or the piercing stars
on the papery sky.
A single footfall
nudges its waters
into oceanic life:
an efflorescence
of dental krill,
flecks of silver cartilage,
filaments of hoki,
tufts of sporing curd
and spongy tags of bone
migrate around the
wobbling globe
of the autumn moon
with the eyes and eggs
of fighting prawns,
all small enough to hide
in the reefs of her teeth
and those of her clients.

# Metro to Grasshopper Hill

No impossible words here:
Cristobal, Cuauhtémoc,
only an insect motto'd
in neon and plastic
guides us underground
through a sea of faces
towards our end of the line,
the word you told us of –
Chapultepec, hill
of the grasshoppers.

And here, so you say,
Aztec emperors came
out to summer palaces,
the floating butterflies
alight upon their
bangled arms;
poets and painters
(you'd have us believe)
listening to the music
in the grass, so far
from the gaily painted
pyramids of blood.

In the traffic island
which is Chapultepec
the roads are up,
and the menagerie
floating on the lake
contains the usual jokes:
black swans paddle
the soapy waters,
Tlaloc the rain god,
driven from his state,
stands dolefully
at the edge of the highway.

The drought broke
when he moved, and was
sufficient for all the people.
For me there is
only coincidence;
this bright chapulin
carrying me back through
the crush of bodies,
a simple guarantee
in Aztec plastic
for the name of the place:
Chapultepec

# Galileo's Watch

It moves! It moves!
His gloved hand tracks across
the empty continent of paper
at the rate of glaciers
cutting schists to alps
up in the Valtellina.

Out here the possessive apostrophe
is only a drop in the ocean.
Even the indigo sworl from his nib,
which resembles a question-mark
as much as the cold Peruvian current
licking the kink in the Andes,
must, like the worst depression,
obey the corkscrew laws of hemispheres.

In my Vallambrosan childhood
the leaves fell as fast as feathers,
the two clocks ticked different times
as I watched them swing, this way and that,
and the leaves fell with regularity
through my Vallambrosan childhood.

As I wait for this jewelled hand,
the Horn of Africa slides towards Arabia,
narrowing the Red Sea by just one inch
in a Biblical life-time.
I've watched its minute progress now
for almost three hundred and
fifty nine years – and I'm sure:
It moves! It moves!

# Minik

We took all our iron from the stars.
Meteorites brought us bear, whale, and walrus,
moose, elk, and fresh herds of caribou.
We turned the seal into warm liver,
snug pants, combs and chiselled amulets,
made it skim the water once again
housed in the taut frame of the kayak.

When they took away our heaviest stones
they carried us along with them too.
We spent all winter huddled in useless overcoats,
lodged in the down-town museum
beneath glass cabinets filled with harpoons,
wasted sinews and ancient arrow-heads
until the common cold took all of us.

When I came back home at eighteen
I was a useless go-between. Words stuck in my throat.
Inuktitut had frozen up on me.
I had to relearn all the verbs to hunt,
to cut, to skin, to fillet, and to chafe
if I was to get back to the body of my father:
his clean bones laid out beneath the icy glass.

As I sit in the shadow of the Iron Mountain,
I try to explain how fast their special knives
worked through my father's wasted flesh,
how much they sliced away to make a *specimen*.
And as I sit and stutter at the polar stars
I hear the down-town lights begin to speak to me
out of the great warm cliffs of Manhattan.

# Amik

We fed solidly on bear grease and the flesh of dogs,
then sweated ourselves inside the makeshift lodge.
My pores flooded the hollows of my collar-bones
and I went down, down, to the bottom of the pool,
past shining aspens, the drift-wood and the dead-wood
beyond the dark beds of freshwater clams
and the rotting stacks of ancient summer leaves
beyond the wriggling ooze of the unnamed,
past all things living, down to the raw earth,
and I cried out in the darkness for some breath,
to pull my worthless pelt back up towards the sun.
My chest aches as an unknown limb launches me
towards the dancing surface of the creek.
A chessaquoy of hawk-bells rattles in my head.
My wounds are seared with punk-wood
and a herb as close as any to old English box.
I was John Long. Now I'm Amik, the beaver.

## Mimicries

Starlings in the sixties
aped the simple bell
of a phone in the hall,
the surge of bath-water
roaring past the plug,
the ripping and zipping
when skipping stations
on a red transistor,
the fuzzy rise and fall
of sitcom laughter
muffled in the eaves.
And through the seventies
and eighties, they moved
along with us within
their own migrations,
as each elaborate alarm
sang through the electric range
of sounds for house and car,
punctuating our sleep
and suburban dreams.
And now I can hear
from the empty lounge
on what I thought was standby
the repeat of a documentary
telling me that keas
have started using
their parrotty beaks
to peel chrome from cars,
and to burgle the burrows
of helpless mutton-birds.

And in the rainforest
just north of Brisbane
the Superb Lyrebird has gone
beyond its natural limit
of twenty local songs
and for the pièce de resistance
of its theatrical display
now includes the click and whirr
of the naturalist's final shot
and the regurgitating rev
of the logger's chain-saw.

# Last of the Race

*Ectopistes Migratorius*

## I

They were as numerous as fish.
When they came in at sun-down
they made a noise like a gale
passing through the rigging
of a close-reefed vessel.
The torrent rolled overhead
out of the range of a gunshot
for a full three days at least
and the air was full of odor.
The light of noon-day was eclipsed.
Their lime loaded the trees like snow
and the ground was strewn with limbs.
All was uproar and confusion.
Under their collapsing nests
the hogs fattened on greasy squabs.
We rendered them down to oil.

## II

I heard sleigh bells in the deep woods.
When I left the wigwam in the morning
an army of horses advanced towards me
with the rumble of an approaching storm.
Yet the day was clear and calm.
As the unbroken front of pigeons
passed through high trees and underbrush
they seemed to overturn each leaf.
I was a statue in the cedar-boughs.
They fluttered all around me, lighting
on my head, my shoulders, and my hands.
I tried hard to understand their language
and why they all chatted together,

fluttering their half-spread wings in
convenient crotches of the trees,
wooing each other with bell-like notes.


## III


I'm left with this grey photograph –
Martha caged in Cincinnati:
the last of her race, 1914.
I leaf through all the pointless details:
the obtusely pointed tail-feathers,
the golden, coppery-bronze neck,
an arbitrary, cinnamon-rufous spot,
the female's pale lake-red feet and legs,
the male's scarlet-vermilion iris
(an excess of hyphens and parentheses)
the livid flesh of his blank eye-space.
I range through all its ideal landscapes,
bursting poke berries, hips, and cherries
from Keewatin to Nova Scotia,
from Kansas down to Mississippi.
I feed on mast and drink secreted curd.

# A Blackcap in Bute Park

Why insist on the song of a bird?
when the usual trees form its green vault,
and a regular drone of traffic maintains its pulse,
composing a scene that is scarcely memorable.

Why insist on the song of a bird?
unless to compare it with the gradual harnessing,
the shifts and shocks before the engine finds its gear,
and makes the separate lines of the road all one.

Why insist on the song of a bird?
when it fills the black space between each sound
with a lively warning of its absence –

unless to recall its silver note.

# The Armley Hippo

*I knew that bones as big as this*
*could not be good Christian bones.*
*I tried to picture to myself*
*Mr Denny's 'Great Northern Hippo',*
*but my poor brain could make nothing*
*of it, except a broken sacrum.*
*I laboured to articulate*
*dorsal and cervical vertebrae.*
*But I couldn't get the fragments of pots*
*and the cracked querns out of my head.*

The mud felt good on their backs.
They slipped into the unnamed Aire
and the carbon-dated
Ipswichian interglacial:
three adults (one aged) and a calf.
In sheltered parts of West Yorkshire,
the cave-lions, the sabre-tooths
and the straight-tusked elephants
finished their usual business.
Aurochs carried on in the meadows.

After that ordinary morning
digging in Longley's brickfield,
he saw Saxons in his mind's eye
passing by on the other side
of the Stanningley high-road,
and he was forced to make way
on the Wortley/Armley border
for Romans in cruel sandals
skipping to the main event:
aerialistes at the Hippodrome.

# The Great Belzoni

Doubled up as acrobat at Sadlers Wells,
he stunned the punters with his waterworks:
Trafalgar, the Armada re-run on ice.
Type-cast in Jack The Giant-Killer,
his body locked into The Human Pyramid.

His new pump outdid old Archimedes'
slow screw, but still wouldn't sell.
So all night he performed fireworks
and electric shocks in the seraglio
with Ibrahim Pasha and the Irish lad.

Six foot seven and *à la Turk*,
he rafts up mother Nile to Karnac,
Abu Simbel and the temple of Jupiter Ammon,
a bronzed athlete among djins and gentlemen
speculating on the ancient Berenice.

He sleeps with mummies at Gournou and Qurna,
his ears, eyes, and throat clogged
with flesh-dust and the looted papyri.
At Giza he unlocks the third pyramid
and has the colossus stacked for Henry Salt.

Red granite Rameses II
keeps his cool in the British Museum
despite the hole through his right breast.
Amenhetep III leans to one side in the sand,
Belzoni tattoed proudly on his chest.

# Heathcliff's Kagemusha

The new signs were beautiful
and conveniently graffiti-proof.
In early summer the fingerposts
blazed the clean calligraphy
across the fabulous moorland;
chapters fell neatly into places,
paths unravelled themselves
with the assurance of a critic.
Swallows skimming the harebells
were English Willow Pattern lovers.

The peace was shattered in autumn.
Directors sat in their canvas chairs
waiting for battle and bad weather.
On the remote ridges of their vision
they saw the flickering of insects
change into the lava-flow of armies.
Narrators lost their nerve and fled;
servants hid behind their screens
and messengers flitted between fortresses
like the ghosts of what would happen.

Was it in Gondal, Angria or Osaka
that at least two sets of Cathys
set out across this no-man's land
only to find that no, they were not
this monster Heathcliff after all?
And where was the familiar stand-in,
the exiled Scouser or the Irishman?
The part could not be played
by any illiterate peasant,
especially one called Kagemusha.

Local glaziers who could make
nothing out of Lockwood's dream
complained at each rake of the wrist
across the imaginary glass.
There were tip-offs about trip-wires.
On the black market puppies went sky high
and on clear nights some people
swore to flights of burning arrows
and one bad angel falling,
falling close to the earth.

# The Nondescript

And so he went in search of curare,
wourali, woorara, urali, unrari,
losing himself among the complex
arteries of the mangroves and lianas
where he learnt the habits of ant-eaters,
the reverse gait of the three-toed-sloth,
and the gentlemanly art of travel
on a twelve foot grinning cayman.
From the Macushi and the Ancoway
he found how one small spike
could make a large dog slide into death
while still barking at strangers.

Twice he queued hours for a glimpse
of the blood of St Januarius
liquefying in the heat of Naples,
and with the same fascination
had mice, rabbits, cats and dogs
and a host of obliging asses,
slide casually from life to death.
Poor Jenny, the first gorilla
ever to die in Warrington,
was cured and then set up
(with ass's ears) as Martin Luther.
Nothing was ever simply stuffed.

Old miners swore blind they'd
seen birds of paradise stalking
the wooded outskirts of Wakefield.
But Walton Hall was so fully blown
that there was nothing left in it.
Tame herons were shot upon their nests,
hounds tore through the smiling game,
and fire consumed his scribbled notes.
He left behind 'The Nondescript'
or wild man of noble countenance,
which good scientific opinion identifies
as the very arsehole of a howler.

# My Crypt Hand

When my heart raced ten and a half miles
from Shibden up to Blackstone Edge
my words flew faster than the mail,
too fast, I know, I spoke too fast
like one I've met with in a dream
your look of shame went through my speech
and I felt an iceberg on my breast.
When you moved into marriage
I would not stop it for the world,
having no world to give in return.
I was not born to live alone:
I said *I've a pain in my knees, M,*
*a pain in my knees*, knowing how to please,
loving you softly, gentleman-like.

You little ween this ink shed of my pen:
I will not give you heart's-ease,
sweet allison, Venus's looking-glass
or even the dwarf passion-flower
to make up your northern nosegay.
These words keep myself from myself,
they oil the soft cog of my heart
which I've washed, again and again,
in corrosive sublimate.
Think only of Fontainebleau grapes
and clean Normandy pears
as my body rumbles back to Halifax
from Terfliz in the dusty Caucasus.
I give you this, my crypt hand.

## It's one of your bitten apples.

(Dorothy Wordsworth's *Grasmere Journal*)


I find it in the space of days
I'm left to busy myself in.
O my darling, I can hardly
bring myself to throw it away:
its pips are like robins' eyes,
and the red skin has smudged
the flesh beneath quite pink.
From its damp, crystalline grooves
I find I am able to form
the distinct impression of your teeth.
O my darling, listen to it
splutter among the fading coals.

# Wertherisms

The old tree
　　　in the same old place.
The canary
　　　pecking both our lips.
Your nail
　　　grazing the cuttle-fish bone.
Grit in my teeth
　　　from kissing your letter.

# After Montaigne

When dace shoaled in the Dordogne
and then exploded on his retina

When the small white heart of a radish
lodged and burned in his chest

When his tongue, like a loyal hound,
searched his gum for the familiar tooth

When the spine of the book in his hand
was all the weight of his friend

When the Tupinamban shivered and coughed
on the cobbles in old Rouen

it was always after Montaigne,
his quicksilver self already split and running
before the wonder of the next question.